Last Day of My Face

I0895256

Winner of the Iowa Poetry Prize

Last Day of My Face

James Shea

University of Iowa Press | Iowa City

University of Iowa Press, Iowa City 52242
Copyright © 2025 by James Shea
uipress.uiowa.edu
Printed in the United States of America
Printed on acid-free paper
Design by Sara T. Sauers

No part of this book may be reproduced or used in any form or by any means without permission in writing from the publisher. All reasonable steps have been taken to contact copyright holders of material used in this book. The publisher would be pleased to make suitable arrangements with any whom it has not been possible to reach.

Library of Congress Cataloging-in-Publication Data
Names: Shea, James, author.
Title: Last Day of My Face / James Shea.
Description: Iowa City: University of Iowa Press, 2025. |
Series: Iowa Poetry Prize
Identifiers: LCCN 2024047402 (print) | LCCN 2024047403 (ebook) |
ISBN 9781685970161 (paperback) | ISBN 9781685970178 (ebook)
Subjects: LCGFT: Poetry.
Classification: LCC PS3619.H3997 L37 2025 (print) |
LCC PS3619.H3997 (ebook) | DDC 811/.6—dc23/eng/20241021
LC record available at https://lccn.loc.gov/2024047402
LC ebook record available at https://lccn.loc.gov/2024047403

For DT

Contents

Last Day of My Face

Sun Broker

Lifeguards can't save themselves
from their own wasting.

What's my record
of attending to the world?

A mute pool in winter.

Is wisdom efficient?

The sun's beams reach
the patio in a tie.

What I need is a continuous ray of light at my side.

A chance to make up
for the luxury of not understanding.

Poor Memorial

It's difficult to point away
from what's all around you.
Dusk among the Sunday people,
leaves fumbling the breeze.
I forfeit any claim to live alone
as one does not, or rather
as one does, but thinks not.
I cannot see myself without
conjuring the vision of no other person:
an empty flat, negative
of where we once lived,
as if even our ghosts were gone.
The seasons outgrow themselves,
break off into a fifth season.
I stand behind glass, staring
at the final leaves, frail divers
curled in upon themselves.

Motion

Sometimes when a tram passenger
looks out the window, a companion
places a hand on her shoulder.
The bell dings at the stop.
No one gets off and wind
enters every window of the carriage.
Scaffolding sways around an office building.
With her hair tied back
the passenger looks down at her lap.
The companion says something brief in his language.
He has never seen a film
that did not contain sound.

Limited Eclipse

I sit at my desk, the wind outside

dismantling the pasture. Skull, my pillow.

Moonlight bisected by the window,

past my shadow, my past, the future:

a street of houses without doors.

The evening descends and lingers

in those moments when talking feels

more desolate than the night. Walk in a circle.

Forgive the night. Know the purpose

of self-confidence. Something anonymous

in the way I've presented myself tonight,

an idea best approached by long-distance

correspondence or a shout from a field

very far afield. I take out my death

and lay it bare. Whittle myself to sleep.

Finish Line

What are they whispering along the telephone wires?

Whose names are they calling among themselves?

There was no subtlety to their departure.

It was to the point: the point of their departure.

One of them left in the wake of the others,

and in the leaving, left a map of its wake.

An ending that made us recall its very origins,

recombinant genes in the wayward leaves.

A crow can recognize a face and speak in dialect.

A crow has hundreds of words from which to choose.

Hardwired

It's an elderly morning,

the oldest one to date,

three handsome dogs,

triplets, walking loosely

with their mistress,

hovering above her work,

as if she had a secret,

or an admirer, or she were

an admirer of secrets,

trees with mops of leaves,

I'm thinking of the last time

I ever climbed a tree,

and why I ever stopped,

I prefer the darker hours

before dawn when work

is applauded by sunlight,

I have a strong sense there

is something very official

and something very unofficial

about these workmen,

emerging out of a hatchback.

Enskied

A white
soft coffin
neither flat
nor deep,
only long
and endless.
We live
side by side.

Day by day
a spotless
bliss, not
a speck
except
the sun
without
its shine.

Skidding Meditations

Skidding Meditation

Consciousness is less a stream,
more a neglected meadow.

Skidding Meditation

Everything, therefore,
nothing, arouses me.

Skidding Meditation

The storm spoke
and spoke and
spoke and spoke
and spoke and
spoke to the sea.

Skidding Meditation

Seen as a wren,
a wren advances.

Seen as a panther,
a panther advances.

Seen as a man,
a man demurs.

Skidding Meditation

Why,

the

sky's

right

here,

next

to

our

faces.

A Void's Void

Made my first misstep: didn't fall asleep
until 4 AM, must've been the late coffee,
wide awake with no itinerary, no bedside text,
no tablet on hand, too cold to go downstairs
to start the day over or to unwind it again,
if the dark were a noise, the house would be a clamor,
but darkness is mute, marshaling its power,
absorbing what's around until the slightest sound
alarms, numbers on a clock emit a bluish light,
a beacon fixed in position as if the lighthouse master
died in his sleep, back-to-back action films
didn't prepare me to rest, winding me up like a tick
in the skin, my pre-dreams were movie scenes,
I slept finally and woke as slow as a Zamboni,
sleep, the foreman of my days, instructing me
on how to move, the pace at which I do,
I wrote a poem about it, a page filled with periods.

This Time of Hour

The Palouse can be coral green,
can be endless, can be disobedient,
the wind can hiss over the hills,
a cloud edge can abut the horizon,
John can be beside me, driving,
or he can have the passenger view,
a landscape can be pregnant with elephants,
dusk in a photograph can be dawn.

That's That

Certain words I dislike.

Ooze. Lozenge. Other words

I love. Katydid. Bumblebee.

Take *that*, for instance,

how it comes fat from the mouth,

nowhere to elide it (massage it).

It's a pronoun (that's what I like),

a conjunction (that I might love),

an adverb (that much),

an adjective (that word

sounds like what it stands for:

is-ness). This is quieter,

less of a claim. I defer

to the sure sense of things.

That's how I approach catastrophe.

Extraordinary Means

Her face a face I had to face again,
her lips on the receiver, feet on the floorboards,
long walks in the house while I'm on the phone
don't count as exercise, a common trait
of cranes on this side of the river is that
they often look back toward the other side
of the river, yellow-brown eyes, she
caught attention, I'm confused by their hue,
she keeps inventing names for herself
every time we meet, distracted as I am
by what's about to present itself, a rider
on a motorcycle passes low to the ground,
unsure how to put myself in the frame
with other people, or to have my name
spoken by a famous person, I'm uncertain
about a stall, it's not for nothing I've arrived,
it's not for something either, it's for some
thing I will give away, celeriac, shallots,
an onion with green shoots, tiny garlic,

one lady had so many eggs, I bought some

to make her glad, once a virgin to aches

of any nature and suddenly a veteran.

Fresh Report

I am here in

the disaster area,

the prescribed

zone of the disaster,

so for those of

you not here,

please be assured

that you are not

experiencing

a disaster for only

those in the radius

of the disaster can

anyone be said

to be suffering

from the disaster.

Setting My Worry Against These Trees

Walking amid variables of snow

Looking at (the) fretwork in the leaves

Smelling a backyard fire midday

Sleeping beside a coup inside an app

Two-Body Problem

Toes are the last to go
when you're dead-dead,
so far from the central
nervous system, so far
from the cerebellum
that departs first, so far
from the valves of the
heart—toes are the last
to know, and for that,
I am in solidarity with
my toes, the little ones
who shall outlast me.

Soft Tank

I dub everything in my own voice.

My mouth never matches perfectly with what I am saying.

I'm sorry.

Life can be life-like, if you like life.

The winner in the winner's circle is always the circle itself.

Can't see that star in the sky?

It's like someone left a flashlight on in the bottom drawer.

Last night, it rained inside a mall.

There's very little crime here, but there could be a war.

Times

I saw the streetlight turn on from my bedroom window,

it was dusk, the sun behind the hills still casting

a white glow against the remains of a backlit sky,

like the sky in Magritte's painting of men falling anonymously,

two streaks of cloud masking part of the air,

twin lights twitched on silently, not overly

noticed, but I observed them in my quietness,

side by side like the headlights of a tiny car

in the trees, nestled together in a shimmer,

steady in their extension by steel from the telephone pole,

the bulbs will bloom for hours, I'm inclined

to sit here and watch until they flick off at dawn,

the only action is the swirl of gnats, not sure

if they see me as some totem, too, a measure

of themselves in some small way this evening time,

they may view me as a single brightness, or two,

less steady than their spotlight, my audience,

from far enough away many lights may look as one.

Fissure

A white stoat in the woods,
graceful and inquisitive,
part *spiritus*, its pulsing heart
nearly visible under its fur,
squirrels in every direction,
unashamed of hunger, snow
melted as if it were never
possible for the earth to be
covered in anything but
sunlight, an alien deer
sees me, my head fits into
the hollow of a tree, sundrops
on my neck, hard to stand
how still a deer can stand.

Recovery Time

A pool of trees in a meadow:

devoicing me.

A book as a sort of passageway,

a way of passages to sort out thoughts,

passages that point a way out.

I'm a swimmer in the hills,

miles away from any pool or pond.

Foothills as footnotes to the sky.

Nature doesn't slide back into place.

After Ma Zhiyuan

Electric valley, a little wind, indefinite clouds.
An old snail, two monkeys, 6-inch moth on the balcony,
coral-green trees, a bus down the mountain, AC.
Traveler without teeth in the middle of a private street.

Saccade

Grandmother's funeral rites: bad vaudeville.

The binocular salesman had an owl-like face.

My signature is a zigzag.

A few new circumstances can change the future.

The future can change the past.

Something inherently elegiac about reversals.

God is infinite, like money.

I can't say anything accurate and universal at the same time.

Except that everyone sleeps.

The new normal is an ancient strange.

Join my company: pay's at half pay.

Only adults giggle nervously.

I sit at the bar, fingering my iPad.

Hang tight means to hang loose.

Writing a poem is like the moment in a musical when people
go suddenly from talking to singing.

The sea of time entails an oarsman.

The sea of time entails an astrolabe, a skiff.

Rich kids don't drown, I heard once.

I want a God that humans can punish.

Sober at 6 AM

The dreams I don't recall
are the most egregious,
the ones I remember also profane,
what does my mind want me
to think? I wake up and
turn on the radio immediately
to control the anxiety
in the house, like a thermostat,
a voice deep, raspy, sexual
in its approach, cold mornings
keep me in bed longer than I want
or rather I revise my wants,
I command cobwebs from here,
I order flies around,
I instruct the dust.

Unbecoming

The sun: whited out.
The cloud: whited out.
The moon, the star—
this sky insists on effacement.

What's to look up to?
A blinding light—
well, it's here now,
the nothingness that was.

I like gradations of white:
beige, chalk, opaline,
snow folded into the scene,
a cloud made of debris.

Poor Ear, Mine Own Instrument

A note held for a lifetime,

an experimental sound

at a constant pitch as if I were

constituted by piercing.

Emergency Chandelier

I split myself in half.

All I could see was

one third of myself.

I tried to imagine

an account of what

had befallen me:

a hacking attack.

I must unsettle these

bones inhabiting me,

idiosyncratic turns

of words that pinpoint

a personality, show me

who's the who who's

speaking, here, in the

cough of a shadow.

Archangel

I spoke against

the circumference

around me, but

I was unheard of.

When it came

to the masters,

I was unread.

They didn't read me.

I hope to make

a good companion

out of myself

after I'm dead.

One Night

My mother held me as a baby.
I felt landlocked in her arms,
situated under a sail inside my head,
alarmed at my broken alarms.

Tin Foil

A crow fell into a bucket.

I didn't feel like eating.

I ordered three drinks.

There was bread and I ate of it.

I was almost almost no one.

I heard the waiter's patter.

Tell the sun I'm done with it.

All the constellations, too.

I'm willing to start over.

Tell the sun I'll take it back.

Tell the constellations, okay.

Guest Speaker

Scab on the back of my heel,

renewed each time I walk in the woods,

spinal discord, that wine at vespers.

I've a misprint on my fingertips.

Is it beer thirty? asked my neighbor.

I took his query as an inquiry into time,

not an invitation to break grapes.

I'm as present as it gets.

Never a reckoning without a wreck.

Mowed my patch of grass in ten minutes flat.

Boss of the lawn. Master of dandelions.

Made a pattern in the sliced blades,

not dead, mind you,

but scaled back in half or more,

invited to return unto me.

What's undone in the yard

remains undone in the mind for some.

Neighbor's hug, a momentary swaddle.

The Station of Prince Edward

There I was at my dining room table
watching you, some clad in black,
and me, me toggling between screens
like a NASA operator in the control room

or the pilot of an underground drone
as umbrellas prodded uncles with hammers
and green police raced down stairs,
while an announcement pleaded for an hour.

Reporters held their cameras in the scrum
and I could have been anywhere but there—
streaming felt like a strange act of love:
to be held by the mind at all times

as you youngsters sprayed by the state
would memorialize the said-to-be dead.
I'm a witness to all this, I told no one.
I'd watch a live-feed of the Crucifixion.

Equipoise

Begin with the formal properties of a ghost:

you seem bound in mystery and loneliness.

I mean bound in mystery and openness,

for loneliness is a kind of openness.

No one's as simple as one would like to be.

This might be the tipping point into happiness,

riding softly into the numinous landscape.

So much for private swallows of water.

We jumped at the first blush between us.

The Womb I Knew

Get inside, he said.
I marveled at its size:
30 feet high and large
enough for 40 men.
Get your sword
and find a spot.
I hate the dark.
I wouldn't say so,
hoisting myself up
on its leg. I sat
near the haunches.
Built in three days
by a master
carpenter, it had
fur on its ribs,
sun-goldened
and clean of slivers.

Chosen by lot,
we heard the voices
of women, maybe
our wives, seized
and suffering.
Our spies said
it was only a ruse.

The men filed out
by a single rope
under night's cover—
I stayed back,

hiding twice: once
from the enemy,
once from comrades.

We were charged
with opening the gates
and murder, but
I confess I remained
in the ass of the ass.
I heard the screams,
indistinguishable cries.
I saw through cracks
mothers wandering,
kissing the doorposts.

Voyage

Whenever I watch a black-and-white film
I think of how all the extras are dead,
I don't think about the stars this way,
they are larger than life on the screen,
shown in close-up, best lit, the film
a testament to their afterlife, but those
extras sadden me with their walk-ons,
cameos of the unknown, they still exist
in some manner here before me, but
in the brevity of their appearance
they are vigorously alive and gone—
a vitality at doing nothing in particular,
not drawing too much attention, quickly
cast aside, that's who I am off camera,
were the director to pan suddenly to me
on my couch—missed more than the stars,
for they have no lines, no special directions,
just told to act naturally without words.

Wake

Shirt came to mourn my chest.

Shoes, the arches of my feet.

Cufflinks, my wrists. Hat, my head.

Socks, my toes, and buttons, my fingers.

Tie came to mourn the nape of my neck.

Belt, my waist. Jacket, my shoulders.

Glasses, my temples and bridge of my nose.

Underwear came and cried at the casket.

Underwear, who knew me best.

Father to Be

Father with a lisp, father with a shovel,
father working in the yard, squinting
as if to indicate he might know me,
father who coaches teenage girls,
father who runs at his own pace,
father who washes his dishes immediately,
father who rides his bike to the olive oil shop,
father whose wife is taut at the mouth,
father who drinks syrup from the bottle,
father who tells jokes about a chicken
in order to roast it, getting a round of salmonella,
father who eats the crispy bits while cooking,
father whose daughters are in a special school,
father who bought a rabbit for his kids,
rabbit that's fat as a bulldog,
rabbit that reminds me of a dinner in China,
rabbit that didn't survive the stew,
rabbit that made me sick at the rabbit restaurant,
rabbit that led to diarrhea at the dorm,
rabbit that made me think I was going to die,
rabbit of no accountability, rabbit that may
have been a show rabbit displayed for patrons,
while the real rabbit was old and expired.

Bicycles

I confirm
that I am
not a bot.
I confirm
that I am
not a bot.

How many
times a day
do I have
to confirm
that I am
not a bot?

I'm a bot
that I can
confirm.
I'm a bot
that I can
confirm.

Immobile Sun, Immobile Moon

Watch me as the one who turns,

hiking toward private property,

decibels within my inner ear,

some things rot from the outside,

some from the inside,

when the sky's blue like this,

it doesn't matter how cold it gets,

safety blue, indisputable blue,

a portion of my self-knowledge

resides within another person,

dust on the radiator I can smell it burning.

Open-Source Apology

There's a rotating restaurant on top of that building.
Everyone looks up.
It doesn't seem to be moving, are you sure?
Yes, I've eaten there myself. It moves very slowly.
Everyone looks up again.
I don't see any movement.
Well, fix your eye on something and see if it moves.
Yeah, I did and I don't see anything happening.
I'm telling you it's a rotating restaurant.
Maybe they're closed and not rotating now.
But I can see people near the window.
It must be open because the lights are on.
Well, it's not moving for me.
There's an abandoned swimming pool at the top.
And the glass elevator is amazing.
You can see the entire city rise up from it.
Sometimes I just take the elevator for the view.
I say, Oh, sorry, I'm on the wrong floor, and go back down.

Runner-Up

Look, a hill comes to rest at his feet,

a hill with the features of a hill,

dusk arrives before the dinner hour,

he compresses what he wants to do,

clever action hero, weak but steely,

he likes a yard with nooks and crannies,

they were right to laugh, and he right

to smile, carrying his young daughters

in both arms up the hill to the house,

them giggling and him charging up

after the hike, how he maintains his days,

dusk collapses him into uncertainty,

now about to render this in such a way

that it's admissible, his son's outdoor

constructions won't last past a day,

his house is dark in winter, darker still

when he wakes up later each day.

The Withheld Detail of the Dream

A pause on my lips—

you fill in what you feel.

Failed Self-Portrait

She smiles in parts, has a story
she can only tell the first sentence of.

1

I've made a sort of makeshift
sense of ourselves,

cohabiting with the cranes
on the windward side of the river,

coming in in waves,
often in pairs, settling in a few inches of water,

thoughts scattering upon the sky,
crepuscular firmament, recognizing myself

too late in its disappearance.
Still, it's kind and sweet

to think I outlived this moment,
even if only for a moment.

Diminished wing,
dead pine in my apartment.

Looking out the window,
waiting to renew a thought

unreturned, I imagine the totality
of the grandest canyon,

so untouched there's no need
to return. Here, women have been known

to go into deepest mourning
for their own relatives or those

of their husbands, or for people,
perhaps, whom they have never seen,

and have remained for seven
or ten years, constantly in black;

then, on losing a child
or a relative dearly loved,

they have no extremity of dress
left to express the real grief.

Outside my apartment, I see two women
showering in the blue light

of a second-story window.
I should continue walking,

but I want to watch discretely,
accept this invitation from life.

It's the nature of profanity
to weaken a bit as it goes.

One or two raindrops are enough
to claim it's raining. You pick me up

from work, smiling inside your mouth,
leaving pieces of me all over:

in the passenger seat,
in the alleyways, among the cattails.

In the yard, an invisible giant
kicks up leaves in his wake,

brushing treetops and treesides
with his shoulders. Undulating branches:

a tree in the wind,
a stand-up drunk.

Sturdy ladybug:
a thimble-sized turtle with personality.

An antelope: don't look up yet (now).
Ah, you've startled him away.

2

I want to set life apart
and examine it, consider its particulars,

but I am swept up. Your turning
of these pages blows a wind upon me.

I feel moved by a small car.
The urge to make love indiscriminately

seems understandable. I've always
enjoyed the architecture

of good times. Tomorrow
is a partial and promised gift.

On a highway in Iowa
I hurtle over a turtle at 75 mph.

It survives my passover. A woman
may wear mourning all her life

if she chooses, but it is a question
whether in so doing she does not

injure the welfare and happiness
of the living. A mistake at the party

leads me to introduce myself to you.
Kindness at first glance.

I speak of hope, but never
with a grin. A glass possesses

the light; no, the light passes
through the glass, whereby

the glass admits the light.
Someone lies to the police about me.

It's just me and my suitcase.
I run out. The sirens sound.

The birdcalls fall silent.
And then I really run out.

I approach a man-made lake,
my shirttails blowing ahead of me.

Anarchists in the capital,
sleeping inside their offices,

bound in cuffs. The management
of the hands in company seems

to embarrass young people greatly.
This comes from the false modesty

which induces them to suppose
they are the observed

of all observers. Don't be alarmed.
I hold no answers, only secrets.

3

Everything is happenstance,
that is, an instance of happening:

there's so much mist/fog/low-clouding
that the mountains haven't quite

revealed themselves utterly yet
and may never do so. A couple of times

I swear there's been part of a cloud
passing at my feet. Ascending

a mountain is usually triumphant,
but when the view is obscured

and you have to start looking inward,
it feels less like a victory.

My necklace drags attention to my chest.
We sit in the warm interior of an old restaurant.

It's desolate in a good way.
Does my dress make *you* look bad?

My admixture of humor and seriousness.
I'm one with whatever.

I'm not saying you should do bad things.
I'm saying if you don't put yourself

into situations in which you could
do bad things, you'll never know

if you're really good or not.
We'd met amid the coin and laundry.

My spotlight turns on itself.
(A couple of folks looking

at their shoes.) I know you to be
more emotionally nimble than me,

but less sure of it. This gives me
a thin advantage. In your eyes,

even the moon is not bright,
nor the stars pure. It's my opportunity for tears.

I mount a mirror to my front bumper,
so I'm always driving into myself.

They say when you die, your life
flashes before your eyes,

so you can't see where you're going.
Ah, the loyalty of my breaths,

one following upon another.
Small tufts of snow blowing

in circles, mostly leftward
with the wind, also downward.

4

Soldiers walk in a field
set with mines, walking

each in each other's footsteps,
exactly in each footstep.

The lake rewrites itself in the wind.
The State says, "Hello."

Cameras watching cameras.
I walk under unlit streetlamps,

bringing the thought of cars turning
without warning, the other side

of the state of things,
streets amiss with rain.

Quiet as a stationery store,
I re-dream the past into an area

where I have some authority.
I wondered once as a boy

at the dark shadow
inside a woman's blouse

when she bent down,
thinking it must be a hole

in her chest. My failures take
many forms, not easily summarized.

They begin as a kind of homelessness
of the mind. I am sober-lonely,

watching sunlight play against
the day's things. I'm not one

to shout down the wind. I know
my place alongside the rivers and cliffs.

Oh,
to

write
a

moderately
long

sentence
that

begins
in

my
mind

and
ends

in
yours.

5

I wait on the sun to stir you into me.
Backlit night sky, creatures drawn

on the early maps of stars, one kind
of constellation implicit inside another.

It's quiet for billions of miles.
Templates of planets found within granite,

the interior life of a landscape—
there is a false shame,

which is the very reverse
of true modesty. It has often

proved fatal to the social qualities
of some who have been otherwise

singularly well adapted not only
to receive from society, but

to bestow upon it both distinction
and happiness. I clean my room

until I no longer recognize myself.
I take off my complicated socks.

6

Could this be a half-feeble attempt
to break into my apartment? The guy

outside my door, half knocking,
half prying it open? Could it be

that I'm talking to him now,
keeping him at bay while I call the police?

Could I be the walking widow,
the widow who knows no windows,

the windowless widow,
the widow of wonderment?

I go fishing, get caught up in the waves
keeping me a part of something greater

than a relationship. A warm animal in my lap.
I like living on the road. "War gets its seed

in the home." I often describe love
as trying to draw on a bird.

Tree of cold, solve this intimacy:
on your blouse, half-flowers akimbo.

What has lasted?
Overpass, overpass,

bleak-bright sun,
solve this intimacy.

7

We break up in a small restaurant,
TV in the corner above our heads

like a little angel. I step out to vomit
in the corporate shrubbery.

I want to get outside myself—
like a white van cradling its dent

through the streets. Toward the end,
one detail reveals itself

as not matching up
with the continuity

of the whole, causing me
to wonder about the veracity

of the entire enterprise,
yet I continue to listen,

waiting for the conclusion
to satisfy my wish

for the tale to be true.
(Once the trapdoor existed

I'd fly through it.) I know
heat lightning is a myth.

It's a storm too far away to hear.
I don't know where I'm going

to sleep tonight. I have a number
of reservations under my name.

8

Due to my left-wingéd thinking,
I fall down and type from the fetal position.

I still have our secret friend career
kept with the wherewithal of a beehive.

Bound to fail in the sense that all that's bound
will fail, I look back at my origins,

a mouse without bone structure,
a flight of needles from a tree,

a wish to put my hand
through the computer. I keep

breaking what has broken, as if
to find the part unbreakable.

9

At my office in the city park,
I meet a cemetery gardener. God's

best viewed, he says, in extremely
close proximity. Review the elm tree,

measure it against other natural acts.
Assess the daffodil. I listen to the clouds

whispering themselves apart. Often
I am not permitted to return to a meadow.

If the depth of acknowledgment
of one's failings measures success,

then I am winning in the oddest way.
It's not easy to understand silence,

to gather ice cream in the morning.
Life's a long self-introduction that ends

abruptly. Take this gray dandelion.
I feel like my tattoo has more personality

than I do. Remember the days
when boys were named Montgomery?

I'm sitting at home, staring at things,
wondering why they are not you. I count molecules

until I fall asleep, until there's no dream,
no evidence. (I never sleep to the sound

of myself awake.) I never saw a loon
on the lake, a hawk swooping down.

I putter around until dinnertime. In the city,
I ask for directions and those three girls were so eager!

Sputtering instructions one by one, looking
this way and that, confirming and contradicting.

It's my scooter on the wet pavement.
Rain falls onto my goggles and helmet.

I drive near trucks and curbs. I'm *there.*
I belong everywhere in general. I'd rather not

respond right now. When I need to speak,
I will. Succinctly, and full of sincerity.

I'd rather ramble into the fictions.
People are dying before I can even get to them.

Acknowledgments

Grateful acknowledgment is made to the Vermont Arts Council for its support during the completion of this book and to the following publications in which some of these poems first appeared: *A Public Space, Bennington Review, Conduit, Court Green, Fence, Fleurs des Lettres, Mississippi Review, North American Review, Notre Dame Review, Portland Review, Stand, Stilts*, and *The Volta.*

Iowa Poetry Prize and Edwin Ford Piper Poetry Award Winners

1987 Elton Glaser, *Tropical Depressions*
Michael Pettit, *Cardinal Points*

1988 Bill Knott, *Outremer*
Mary Ruefle, *The Adamant*

1989 Conrad Hilberry, *Sorting the Smoke*
Terese Svoboda, *Laughing Africa*

1990 Philip Dacey, *Night Shift at the Crucifix Factory*
Lynda Hull, *Star Ledger*

1991 Greg Pape, *Sunflower Facing the Sun*
Walter Pavlich, *Running near the End of the World*

1992 Lola Haskins, *Hunger*
Katherine Soniat, *A Shared Life*

1993 Tom Andrews, *The Hemophiliac's Motorcycle*
Michael Heffernan, *Love's Answer*
John Wood, *In Primary Light*

1994 James McKean, *Tree of Heaven*
Bin Ramke, *Massacre of the Innocents*
Ed Roberson, *Voices Cast Out to Talk Us In*

1995 Ralph Burns, *Swamp Candles*
Maureen Seaton, *Furious Cooking*

1996 Pamela Alexander, *Inland*
Gary Gildner, *The Bunker in the Parsley Fields*
John Wood, *The Gates of the Elect Kingdom*

1997 Brendan Galvin, *Hotel Malabar*
Leslie Ullman, *Slow Work through Sand*

1998 Kathleen Peirce, *The Oval Hour*
Bin Ramke, *Wake*
Cole Swensen, *Try*

1999 Larissa Szporluk, *Isolato*
Liz Waldner, *A Point Is That Which Has No Part*

2000 Mary Leader, *The Penultimate Suitor*

2001 Joanna Goodman, *Trace of One*
Karen Volkman, *Spar*

2002 Lesle Lewis, *Small Boat*
Peter Jay Shippy, *Thieves' Latin*

2003 Michele Glazer, *Aggregate of Disturbances*
Dainis Hazners, *(some of) The Adventures of Carlyle, My Imaginary Friend*

2004 Megan Johnson, *The Waiting*
Susan Wheeler, *Ledger*

2005 Emily Rosko, *Raw Goods Inventory*
Joshua Marie Wilkinson, *Lug Your Careless Body out of the Careful Dusk*

2006 Elizabeth Hughey, *Sunday Houses the Sunday House*
Sarah Vap, *American Spikenard*

2008 Andrew Michael Roberts, *something has to happen next*
Zach Savich, *Full Catastrophe Living*

2009 Samuel Amadon, *Like a Sea*
Molly Brodak, *A Little Middle of the Night*

2010 Julie Hanson, *Unbeknownst*
L. S. Klatt, *Cloud of Ink*

2011 Joseph Campana, *Natural Selections*
Kerri Webster, *Grand & Arsenal*

2012 Stephanie Pippin, *The Messenger*

2013 Eric Linsker, *La Far*
Alexandria Peary, *Control Bird Alt Delete*

2014 JoEllen Kwiatek, *Study for Necessity*

2015 John Blair, *Playful Song Called Beautiful*
Lindsay Tigue, *System of Ghosts*

2016 Adam Giannelli, *Tremulous Hinge*
Timothy Daniel Welch, *Odd Bloom Seen from Space*

2017 Alicia Mountain, *High Ground Coward*
Lisa Wells, *The Fix*

2018 Cassie Donish, *The Year of the Femme*
Rob Schlegel, *In the Tree Where the Double Sex Sleeps*

2019 William Fargason, *Love Song to the Demon-Possessed Pigs of Gadara*
Jennifer Habel, *The Book of Jane*

2020 Emily Pittinos, *The Last Unkillable Thing*
Felicia Zamora, *I Always Carry My Bones*

2021 Emily Pérez, *What Flies Want*

2022 Melissa Crowe, *Lo*
Maggie Queeney, *In Kind*

2023 Stephanie Choi, *The Lengest Neoi*
Peter Mishler, *Children in Tactical Gear*

2024 Mackenzie Kozak, *no swaddle*
James Shea, *Last Day of My Face*